Advent Devotions &
CHRISTMAS CRAFTS
FOR
FAMILIES

24 SCRIPTURE REFLECTIONS
& SIMPLE PROJECTS
TO ANTICIPATE CHRIST'S BIRTH

VICTORIA DUERSTOCK

Good Books
New York, New York

Good Books books may be purchased in bulk at special discounts for sales promotion, corporate gifts, fund-raising, or educational purposes. Special editions can also be created to specifications. For details, contact the Special Sales Department, Good Books, 307 West 36th Street, 11th Floor, New York, NY 10018 or info@skyhorsepublishing.com.

Good Books is an imprint of Skyhorse Publishing, Inc.®, a Delaware corporation.

Visit our website at www.goodbooks.com.

10 9 8 7 6 5 4 3 2

Library of Congress Cataloging-in-Publication Data is available on file.

Cover design by Laura Klynstra

Print ISBN: 978-1-68099-648-7
Ebook ISBN: 978-1-68099-678-4

Printed in China

Contents

Introduction

I have always enjoyed family time, especially around the holidays. It is such a blessing to set aside time together to reflect on Christ's birth. What a joy to share some of our family's special projects and reflections with you!

The crafts and devotions that follow are meant to cover a wide variety of ages and abilities. You will find that certain crafts will require a little more attention from older kids or adults, while others are quite simple. You may want to look ahead at the beginning of each week to decide which projects your family will do and what supplies you may need.

There is one devotion and one craft for each day in December leading up to our joyous celebration of the birth of Christ. The weeks follow the traditional Advent themes of hope, love, joy, and peace.

I pray your family will be blessed with time together and time to consider the beauty of what this season means.

HOPE

DECEMBER

1 *Holding My Breath*

The record of the genealogy of Jesus the Messiah, the son of David, the son of Abraham. Matthew 1:1 (KJV)

Just like we look forward to Christmas Day, the Jewish people waited for their King. Their Messiah had been promised but still had not arrived. The waiting went on and on and on. The countdown was so long, in fact, that God was silent to His chosen people, the Jews, *for over 400 years*!

Some of God's people forgot what they were taught. Others remembered and taught their children and their grandchildren all of God's promises. These promises included the one about their coming rescuer and promised King.

At Christmas we celebrate the arrival of that King, the Messiah. We anticipate all the fun of Christmas Day like unwrapping presents, eating favorite foods, and playing games with our families. Advent, the twenty-four days leading up to Christmas, is a reminder for us of how the Jews waited and watched for the signs of their arriving rescue.

This Christmas, as you count down to Christmas Day, remember how the Jews awaited their King all those many years ago!

Dear Jesus, we thank you so much for fulfilling the promise to the Jews and coming to earth to redeem us. Help me remember while I wait for Christmas Day that Christmas is really about this promise fulfilled.

Reflections:

Have you ever been promised something, but you had to wait for it?

_____

_____

_____

_____

What were the Jewish people waiting to be rescued from?

_____

_____

_____

_____

Read Joshua 21:45, Joshua 23:14, and Philippians 1:6. What are some things we learn about God's promises?

_____

_____

_____

_____

Let's Make a Gift! M&M Cookie Mix in a Jar

INGREDIENTS:

- 1½ cups all-purpose flour
- 1 teaspoon baking powder
- ½ teaspoon baking soda
- ¼ teaspoon salt

- 1¼ cups holiday M&M's
- ⅓ cup light brown sugar, packed
- ½ cup granulated sugar
- 1-quart mason jar

DIRECTIONS FOR ASSEMBLING JARS:

1. Combine flour, baking powder, baking soda, and salt in a small bowl. Pour into the bottom of a 1-quart mason jar. You can use a funnel or a rolled paper plate to assist.
2. Top the flour mixture with M&M's, dropping them in lightly, so that they don't sink into the flour.
3. Top the M&M's with brown sugar, and then granulated sugar (use a spoon to carefully scoop the sugars into the jar).
4. Seal with the lid. You can decorate the lid if you want to!

RECIPE TO INCLUDE WITH THE JAR:

M&M Cookies

Each jar makes approximately 20 cookies.

1. In a large bowl, whisk ½ cup of melted and cooled unsalted butter with 1 large egg and 2 teaspoons vanilla extract. Add the contents of the jar and gently stir with a wooden spoon or rubber spatula until combined (dough will be crumbly).
2. Chill for 30 minutes.
3. Form golf ball–sized portions of dough, pressing firmly as you form each ball. Place the dough balls onto baking sheets lined with parchment paper.
4. Bake at 350°F for 8–10 minutes or until the edges are set and the centers of the cookies are still slightly underdone.
5. Place baking sheets on a rack to cool, then use a spatula to remove cookies from the pan. Store in an airtight container.

The Very Best Hope

But when the fulness of the time was come, God sent forth his Son, made of a woman, made under the law, To redeem them that were under the law, that we might receive the adoption of sons. Galatians 4:4–5 (KJV)

Hope is something that we all need. Hope rests in the promise of a future. Hope promises that there are brighter days ahead. Hope helps us to try again and again.

In this passage, we as Christ's followers are reminded of the truth our hope rests in. At precisely the right time in history, God sent Jesus to earth. Just as He had promised and just as the prophets had said! Because of a miracle that only God could do, He made Mary a mother to the Son of God. This was exactly what the Old Testament prophets had said would happen.

Jesus had a very specific purpose for His life. He was the answer to our sin problem, our rescuer, and the only one who could restore our relationship with God to what it was meant to be. Because of this great sacrifice—leaving Heaven's throne and coming to Earth to live and die for us—we can have our sins forgiven and be adopted into His family. This is the ultimate and very best hope fulfilled for us.

Thank you, God, for the gift of your Son. Because Jesus came to earth, I can be filled with eternal hope!

Reflections:

What does Romans 3:23 tell us about sin?

_____

_____

_____

_____

What does Romans 6:23 tell us is the payment due for our sin?

_____

_____

_____

_____

Read the story of Abraham and Isaac and the sacrifice that God provided (Genesis 22:1–18). How does this story compare to the Nativity story?

_____

_____

_____

_____

Let's Make a Gift! Cinnamon Oatmeal Soap

SUPPLIES:

- 2 pounds oatmeal soap base
- 2 teaspoons cinnamon bark essential oil
- Soap molds
- Cooking spray

- Cinnamon sticks (optional)
- Jute (optional)
- Baker's twine (optional)

DIRECTIONS:

1. Cut the soap base into smaller pieces and place it in a microwave-safe dish.

2. Microwave the soap at reduced strength for 30 seconds at a time, stirring in between.

3. Add your cinnamon bark essential oil to melted base and stir well.

4. Spray soap molds with cooking spray.

5. Pour the melted oatmeal cinnamon soap into the molds and allow the soap to set completely.

6. Push out of the mold gently and slice into bars (if needed, depending on mold).

7. Decorate with jute, twine, cinnamon sticks, or whatever you want!

Watch the Signs

Therefore the Lord himself shall give you a sign; Behold, a virgin shall conceive, and bear a son, and shall call his name Immanuel. Isaiah 7:14 (KJV)

Sometimes we don't know which way to go. We have learned to follow the signs that lead us to our destination. We use maps on our phones or navigation systems in the car to get us from one place to another much like travelers of old followed the stars and planets to get them to their destination. We read signs to know what lane to use to check out at the grocery store, when to stop the car at an intersection to avoid an accident, and to spot our favorite restaurants and shops!

In the Bible, there were many times that followers of God sought answers for their questions. They would often beg God to give them a sign. Gideon was one such person in the time of the Judges. He offered up a sheep's fleece and asked God to keep it dry when the ground around was wet with morning dew. He woke up to find that God answered that request. The very next day Gideon asked God once again for a sign, but He reversed his request. God made the fleece wet but kept the ground around it dry. Because God was patient and answered Gideon again, Gideon moved forward in obedience to protect God's people.

In the book of Isaiah, God promised a sign of the coming Messiah to the Jews, and we can rejoice that God kept His promise. A virgin, Mary, did have a son, and He was the one that had been promised through Isaiah about 700 years earlier! The Jews who listened and watched for the signs rejoiced to know that Jesus was the One promised!

Thank you, Jesus, for the signs that you gave us throughout the Old Testament!
I am so thankful you can be trusted to fulfill your promises.

Reflections:

Think about a favorite trip you've taken. What might it have been like if you didn't have any directions or signs to help you get there?

_____

_____

_____

_____

Write out Luke 2:12. What was the sign?

_____

_____

_____

_____

How does it make you feel when someone keeps their promise?

_____

_____

_____

_____

Twig Christmas Tree Ornaments

SUPPLIES:

- Varying sizes of sticks/twigs
- Glue gun and glue
- Green yarn
- Mini pom poms or buttons
- Scissors

DIRECTIONS:

1. Break twigs into two long sidepieces, one short crosspiece, and one small trunk. Glue each piece together with the glue gun.

2. Cut a long length of green yarn and tie one end onto the tree. Wrap the yarn around the tree over and over again, going from side to side and up and down. You can do it first all in one direction and then all in the other direction (as shown next to step 3), or back and forth however you wish (as shown next to step 4). Tie the remaining end of the yarn to the tree after you have built up a green middle.

3. Glue your tree decorations onto the strands of yarn. Try pom poms, buttons, beads, little bells, sequins, or anything else you can think of.

4. Use a yellow pom pom or button for a star on top if you want!

4

Simeon

And, behold, there was a man in Jerusalem, whose name was Simeon . . . waiting for the consolation of Israel . . . Luke 2:25 (KJV)

Simeon lived his life full of hope. He had been taught that the Messiah was coming, and he served in the temple always watching for hope to be fulfilled. Sometimes when we say we hope for something, it's a very shallow thought. Like you say, "I hope I can make the basketball team," but then you never go out to practice. Or you think, "I hope we have cinnamon rolls for breakfast tomorrow," but you never make that suggestion out loud. Hebrews 6:19 compares hope to an anchor. It reminds me that hope is constant and unchanging, no matter the storms we may face.

Being filled with hope means believing with expectation, just like Simeon did. He worked faithfully in the temple doing the work he had been given. When Jesus was born and brought to the temple, Simeon went to the temple. He had been waiting for him and he obeyed the call to go to the temple that day. He knew immediately that He was the Messiah because he had lived for all those years with hope.

We can be filled with hope as well. God shows us that we can trust Him to make all His promises come true.

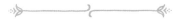

We are so thankful for the birth of Jesus, the Messiah! Thank you, Lord, for being so trustworthy.

Reflections:

Why is comparing hope to an anchor comforting? What does an anchor do?

_____

_____

_____

_____

How can I be faithfully serving right now, at my age?

_____

_____

_____

_____

Can you think of any other promises God makes in the Bible that give you hope?

_____

_____

_____

_____

Stained Glass Nativity

SUPPLIES:

- Contact paper
- Nativity silhouette
- Colorful tissue paper cut into squares
- Scissors

DIRECTIONS:

1. Freehand draw a nativity silhouette or find one online and print. Cut out the nativity. Place contact paper sticky side up. Center your nativity silhouette on top of the contact paper and lay it down.

2. Place squares of tissue paper inside the nativity silhouette to create the look of stained glass.

3. Once the nativity is filled with tissue paper, lay a second sheet of contact paper on top of the entire project. Be careful not to trap air bubbles. Use a credit card to smooth out any bubbles that appear. Trim the excess contact paper with scissors.

4. Hang your stained-glass nativity on a window with tape, or use a hole punch and hang it from a string as a tree ornament.

5 Emmanuel, God with Us

Behold, a virgin shall be with child, and shall bring forth a son, and they shall call his name Emmanuel, which being interpreted is, God with us. Matthew 1:23 (KJV)

Jesus was the promised one, the Messiah come to rescue His people from their sins. But Jesus is also called "Emmanuel," which means "God with us," a truth that brings joy, hope, and peace.

There are days when I feel alone. I've had days when I've cried over friends who hurt me, or when I got picked last for games on the playground. Or even worse days when I have lost a pet or family member. The days when I feel I am all alone, I remember that I am not. Instead I read again the promise of Emmanuel—this truth that Jesus not only rescues me from my sins and promises a home in Heaven one day, but also that He will never leave me alone.

Emmanuel means "God with us." Not "God will be with us in the future," or "God was with us in the past." Both those things *are true*. But the promise that God is with us now helps me to work through my feelings and emotions on the bad days.

Dear Jesus, thank you for being the promised Messiah from the Old Testament and being faithfully with us today and every day.

Reflections:

What does it mean to you that Emmanuel means "God with us"?

_____

_____

_____

_____

Tell about a time you felt all alone.

_____

_____

_____

_____

Read Joshua 1:9 and tell me what promise God gives us about being alone.

_____

_____

_____

_____

Homemade Salt Dough Ornaments

INGREDIENTS:

- 1 cup flour
- ½ cup salt
- ½ cup water
- Plastic straw

ADDITIONAL DECORATING ITEMS:

- Acrylic paint
- Paint brush
- Puffy paint
- Curling ribbon for hanging
- Clear spray paint to seal ornaments
- Food coloring
- Scissors

DIRECTIONS:

1. Preheat oven to 225ºF. Line a baking sheet with aluminum foil and set aside.
2. Mix flour and salt in a bowl. Add water and stir until a dough forms.
3. On a lightly floured surface, knead the dough for at least 5 minutes, continuing to add flour as needed to prevent the dough from sticking. Roll out the dough onto a lightly floured surface about ¼" thick. Use cookie cutters to make different shapes.
4. Place the cutouts on the foil-lined baking sheet and use the straw to put a hole in the top of the ornament.
5. Bake ornaments until dry. Turn over every 30 minutes. Remove from oven and place on parchment paper.
6. Decorate as desired with paints and let dry completely.
7. Coat each ornament with a clear spray to seal it and dry. Do both the front and the back.
8. Cut ribbon and tie a knot in the end. Thread through the hole. And then push knot back through the open end to create a slipknot.

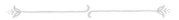

And there was one Anna ... And she coming in that instant gave thanks likewise unto the Lord, and spake of Him to all them that looked for redemption in Jerusalem. Luke 2:36–38 (KJV)

Anna, a devout follower and worshiper in the temple, never missed an opportunity to serve. She was a widow who continued to serve in the temple. She was known for her devotion to fasting and praying. She lived her life in service to the Lord, so it is no wonder at all that she was aware of who Jesus was.

This reminds me that when I follow the Lord by reading my Bible and praying, I will get to know Him so well that when He is at work among us, I will recognize Him. Whether that's in my school, my home, my church, or around the world. God is at work, and we can recognize Him at work as we spend time with Him.

Just like we learn more about our friends when we spend more time with them, this story reminds us that we can get to know Jesus better by spending time reading the Bible and praying!

I thank you God that we can know you because of the Bible. We praise you for being so good!

Reflections:

How often do you read your Bible and pray?

_____

_____

_____

_____

What does II Timothy 3:16–17 say about the Bible?

_____

_____

_____

_____

Do you think that God hears you when you pray? Read I John 5:15 and share what it says.

_____

_____

_____

_____

Stained Glass Ornaments

SUPPLIES:

- Recycled plastic (any clear plastic fruit containers are great!)
- Sharpie markers
- Black construction paper
- Glue

DIRECTIONS:

1. Cut plastic into a circle shape the size of an ornament.
2. Draw an outline straight onto the plastic with a black Sharpie to look like the panels of a stained-glass window.
3. Color in the design using various Sharpie colors.
4. Retrace the black lines again as necessary after coloring.
5. Cut a black paper frame just a little bigger than the plastic ornament. Glue the black paper frame onto the plastic.
6. Punch a hole in the top, add string, and hang on the tree.

LOVE

DECEMBER

7

The Good Shepherd

I am the good shepherd: the good shepherd giveth his life for the sheep. John 10:11 (KJV)

The Bible gives us many beautiful stories about sheep and the shepherd. I don't know if I fully understood these stories until we started raising sheep after we moved to Mississippi. There is so much work that goes into caring for sheep. Every morning and evening, no matter the weather, the kids had to go out and check on them. Many times, the sheep were already crying out for their food and water by baaing in their pens. Food had to be measured precisely or they might overeat and be sick. Water had to be dumped out when it got dirty. The bowls had to be washed because they would get slimy very quickly when the water was dirty. The stalls had to be cleaned out with shovels and hoses so that the sheep would have a clean area to lie down and sleep in. During the spring, sometimes we even needed to bottle-feed the little babies.

It was messy work and sometimes our children didn't really feel like doing it. But they didn't have a choice—the sheep were completely dependent on them. They were their shepherds. Over time the sheep knew the sound of their voices and followed the one they knew cared for them each day.

I learned so much about these Bible verses by watching the sheep we raised. The promise of the Good Shepherd is so rich and deep. He cares for our needs, He protects us, He provides for us, and He prospers us. Because of His great love for us, He sacrificed Himself for us. What a Good Shepherd He is!

Thank you, Lord, for being our Good Shepherd. You care for all of our needs and we thank you!

Reflections:

Read Psalm 23. Which verse is your favorite?

_____

_____

_____

_____

What does it mean that Jesus is our Good Shepherd?

_____

_____

_____

_____

What does "sacrifice" mean?

_____

_____

_____

_____

Lamb Ornament

SUPPLIES:

- 5 or more cotton balls
- 2 mini clothespins
- Hot glue gun and glue
- Craft glue
- Googly eyes
- Black construction paper
- Sharpie marker
- String, twine, or cord to hang the ornament

DIRECTIONS:

1. For large sheep, use 4 cotton balls as the base and glue them with just a little hot glue in a square shape (2 by 2). For smaller sheep, use 2 cotton balls glued back to back.

2. Cut a piece of cord or twine 4–6 inches long and make a loop by tying a knot and hot gluing the knot to the center of the cotton balls. Attach the mini clothespins to the base of the sheep with a little hot glue. Start pulling apart several pieces of cotton until they are fluffy but still connect. Glue the fluffy pieces to the base cotton balls.

3. Freehand draw and cut out a sheep face from the piece of construction paper. Attach the googly eyes with craft glue. Draw the mouth and nose with the Sharpie. Glue with craft glue onto the front of your sheep.

4. Make a whole flock of sheep if you want, or just stick with one.

DECEMBER

Everlasting Love

For I am persuaded, that neither death, nor life, nor angels, nor principalities, nor powers, nor things present, nor things to come, Nor height, nor depth, nor any other creature, shall be able to separate us from the love of God, which is in Christ Jesus our Lord. Romans 8:38–39 (KJV)

It's very hard to imagine and fully understand what the love of God means to us personally. The older I get the more I realize I just don't have the ability to really understand it completely. As a child, I was able to accept things that I didn't fully understand, but as we get older, we can start trying to make God fit our minds. The thing about God is that His ways are higher than our ways and His thoughts are higher than our thoughts (Isaiah 55:8). We are told in the Bible that we simply cannot understand why He does what He does because we are human and not God. No matter how much it doesn't make sense that He loves me sometimes, He says in his Word that He does, and I can believe that.

This love is a love that cannot be broken. This passage in Romans reminds me that there is absolutely nothing in this world that can separate me from God's love. *Nothing.* No matter what is happening today, no matter my hurts and disappointments, no matter how my friends fail me, or I struggle to get through class or my homework, none of those things can keep me from the everlasting and perfect love of God. It's greater than anything that I can understand or explain. It's stronger and richer than anything else. What comfort this truth brings me when I am struggling. When I am afraid and when I don't understand, He loves me no matter what.

Thank you, God, for your love for me. I am thankful that nothing can separate me from your love.

Reflections:

Share a time when you felt loved.

_____

_____

_____

_____

What does I Corinthians 13:13 teach us about love?

_____

_____

_____

_____

How can I show love to someone else?

_____

_____

_____

_____

Scrap Ribbon Tree Ornaments

SUPPLIES:

- Straight sticks or cinnamon sticks
- Ribbons
- Hot glue gun
- Twine
- Scissors

DIRECTIONS:

1. Tie the scraps of ribbon down the twig or cinnamon stick. Don't tie too tightly until all of them have been added and bunched together.

2. Bunch the ribbons as closely together as possible. The ribbons will bend and slightly overlap. Gently tug them into place until you are satisfied with their placement.

3. Trim the ribbon scraps into the shape of a Christmas tree. Hot glue or tie a loop of twine to the top of the tree.

4. If desired, top the tree with a wooden star, yellow button, or any other tree topper you can imagine.

DECEMBER

God Is Love

For God so loved the world, that he gave his only begotten Son, that whosoever believeth in him should not perish, but have everlasting life. John 3:16 (KJV)

The Gospel is the good news that because God loves us so much, He sacrificed His only Son for us. Because God is holy and also loving, He provided a way for us to be rescued. He was unwilling to leave us lost in our sin and separated from Him forever. In His great mercy and kindness, He sacrificed the One whom He loved to die on a cross for our sins, to be buried and to rise again the third day. If we will believe, we can have life everlasting in Heaven one day.

This love doesn't mean that life will be easy. We will experience grief, pain, and loss. But the promise of the Gospel is that this life is not all there is. Joy awaits us in Heaven, and we will be reunited with the One who is love and who loves us dearly. I am so grateful too that we can have joy as we live each day here on Earth. Despite the hurts, God's presence and His promises bring me joy and allow me to develop joy in my heart even when circumstances are not fun!

God, I thank you for the love you give us freely and for the promise of Heaven one day.

Reflections:

Read Matthew 22:37–39. What does this passage tell us we are supposed to do?

_____

_____

_____

_____

What do you think Heaven will be like?

_____

_____

_____

_____

What does everlasting or eternal life mean?

_____

_____

_____

_____

Popsicle Stick Christmas Trees

SUPPLIES:

- 3 green popsicle sticks
- 1 green or brown popsicle stick
- 4" twine
- Sparkly stickers for ornaments
- Foam star stickers (optional)
- Hot glue

DIRECTIONS:

1. Cut the green popsicle sticks into 6 pieces.
    Lengths should be ½", 1", 1½", 2", 2½", and 3".
    Snip both sides of the stick to "score" and then bend to snap apart.
2. Place the full-length green or brown popsicle stick down first. On top of this lay the two ends of twine and glue to the popsicle stick. Add the ½" piece of green popsicle stick across the top and press down all together.
3. Line up the remaining green popsicle stick pieces evenly along the long stick and glue them in place with hot glue. Use hot glue to attach the sticker star (optional).
4. Decorate your tree with the glittery stickers!

10

Sacrificial Love

Fulfil ye my joy, that ye be likeminded, having the same love, being of one accord, of one mind. Let nothing be done through strife or vainglory; but in lowliness of mind let each esteem other better than themselves. Philippians 2:2–3 (KJV)

The kind of love that we are to share with others is one that is always putting others first. I remember learning the acrostic J-O-Y when I was a little girl. **J**-esus first, **O**-thers second, **Y**-ourself last. In our world today it's easy to forget to put others first. Whether we are standing in line to get food or waiting our turn for a fun ride, we often want to go first, but real joy allows others to be first. Playing team sports can be a tough arena to put others first, but a good team player looks for opportunities to benefit the team not only by scoring points himself, but also by including other members in the process by being a good "assister."

Jesus never struggled like we do to make those decisions. He lived as a human being perfectly and when it was His time to make the ultimate sacrifice, He laid down his life willingly. He knew that physical pain was not the only punishment He was facing either. He looked ahead to the cross knowing that he would also have to feel separation for a brief time with His Father because He would carry our sins on His shoulders.

This kind of love is the kind of love required of us when we are called to be like Christ. A couple verses later in this passage we are told to have this mind in us, just like Christ's.

Lord help me love others like you do so that they may learn to love you too!

Reflections:

Read the rest of Philippians 2:5–8. What kind of mind should we have?

_____

_____

_____

_____

What does it mean to you to put others first?

_____

_____

_____

_____

Who could I demonstrate love to this week?

_____

_____

_____

_____

Muddy Buddies Snacks

INGREDIENTS:

- 1 cup chocolate chips
- ½ cup peanut butter
- ¼ cup butter
- 1 teaspoon vanilla extract

- 7 cups Chex cereal
- 2 cups powdered sugar
- 2 cups red and green M&M's

DIRECTIONS:

1. Melt chocolate chips, peanut butter, and butter in a large microwaveable bowl for 30 seconds and then stir. Continue microwaving in 15 second increments, stirring after each time, until chocolate is completely melted. Stir in vanilla.

2. Gently fold in Chex cereal, being careful not to break up the pieces until it's evenly coated.

3. Add powdered sugar to a large zip-top bag and add cereal mixture. Seal the bag and shake well until each piece is evenly covered with powdered sugar.

4. Transfer chow back to a clean bowl and fold in M&M's.

5. Enjoy right away or store in an airtight container.

DECEMBER

11

What's in a Name?

For unto us a child is born, unto us a son is given: and the government shall be upon his shoulder: and his name shall be called Wonderful, Counsellor, The mighty God, The everlasting Father, The Prince of Peace. Isaiah 9:6 (KJV)

Moms and dads everywhere spend a lot of time deciding on their children's names. A lot! Some worry for weeks what they will name their precious baby, and some decide the moment they see their infant son or daughter for the first time. Each name has a meaning and a significance and is special for each one of us. My name means victorious spirit! I have always loved knowing this because it reminds me to persevere!

Sometimes we receive a family name that has a special meaning through the generations, or because someone has good memories of a person with that name and they want us to carry that name and those memories on through time.

The names we read here in this passage remind me that the names of Jesus can remind me of the different reasons I know He loves and cares for me. My friends and family can let me down sometimes, but Jesus never fails. He never disappoints. He never forgets or leaves me out. Each one of His names reminds me how very much I am loved and cared for even if everyone else leaves me behind. I am so thankful for the promises I find in His names.

Thank you, God, for being Wonderful, Counselor, Almighty God, Everlasting Father, and Prince of Peace.

Reflections:

Read Luke 1:31–32. What names are listed here for Jesus?

_____

_____

_____

_____

What does your name mean? If you don't know, look it up.

_____

_____

_____

_____

Why do you think your mom or dad may have chosen that name for you?

_____

_____

_____

_____

Names of Jesus Advent Chain

SUPPLIES:

- Construction paper
- Scissors

- Tape or stapler and staples
- Pen, pencil, marker, or crayon

DIRECTIONS:

1. Cut your paper into 1" x 11" strips.

2. Write one of the names of Jesus on the back of each strip. Alternate colors or keep them all the same. Be creative! See opposite page for some names you can use.

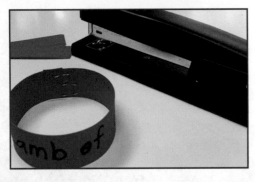

3. Tape or staple your first strip together to make a loop.

4. Thread the next strip of paper through the first loop and staple/tape it closed.

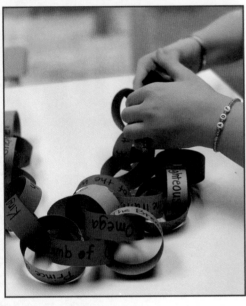

5. Continue doing this, alternating the colors (if desired), until all the strips are gone.

- Emmanuel
- The Root of Jesse
- Prince of Peace
- The Lamb of God
- The Good Shepherd
- The Way, The Truth and The Life
- The Bread of Life
- Alpha and Omega
- Dayspring from on High

- The Head
- Lord of Lords
- Light of the World
- Bright and Morning Star
- The Sun of Righteousness
- King of Kings
- Messiah
- King of Glory
- Savior of the World

- A Precious Stone
- The Builder
- The Vine
- The Son of the Living God
- A Sure Foundation
- The Word
- The Resurrection

12 *The Word Made Flesh*

And the Word was made flesh, and dwelt among us (and we beheld his glory, the glory as of the only begotten of the Father), full of grace and truth. John 1:14 (KJV)

The greatest part of the Christmas story is that God took on our human flesh. Jesus becoming man meant that He had physical and mental limitations living on earth instead of His heavenly home and eventually endured the shame of the rejection of those whom He loved and His death on the cross. He brought love and grace and truth to us.

Heaven came down and lived here. He walked and talked with us. He taught His disciples, had meals together, and healed the sick. He cast out demons, fed thousands with a few small fish and a small amount of bread, and turned the water into wine. He called the outcasts His friends, and He said to let the little children come to Him. He taught that women and children were important, and He made everyone think a little bit more about everything they thought they knew and understood.

Thank you, Jesus, for the miracles we read about in your Word. Thank you for loving and welcoming children into your life.

Reflections:

Read about some of the miracles that Jesus performed (John 2:1–11; Matthew 12:22; and Mathew. 14:15–21 are a few passages). Which is your favorite?

_____

_____

_____

How does it make you feel that Jesus allowed children to come to him? (Matthew 19:14)

_____

_____

_____

How did Jesus treat women and children differently than the rulers of his day?

_____

_____

_____

Mimi's Origami Treat Boxes

SUPPLIES:

- 2 pieces of square paper (Recycled Christmas cards are perfect! The second piece of paper should be ½" smaller than the first. The larger piece is your box lid.)

DIRECTIONS:

1. Place paper pattern-side down, fold in half, and crease. Open your paper out. Turn 90 degrees. Fold in half again. Open out. Your paper should now be divided into 4 squares.

2. Next, fold your paper corner-to-corner on the diagonal to form a triangle. Open it out, turn 90 degrees, and repeat. Fold one of the corners into the center of your paper square. Repeat for the other 3 corners.

3. Take your square, fold the bottom and top edges into the center. Open back out. Rotate 90 degrees and repeat step. Open back out.

4. Lift up 2 opposite triangles and lay them flat.

5. To form the box, lift and fold the sides toward the center. As you pull on the sides, the top triangle will start to pull up. Collapse in the corners and crease.

(Continued on next page . . .)

6. Lift the top triangular flap up and over to form 3 sides of your box. Turn 180 degrees and repeat.

7. Repeat the whole process using the smaller square of paper. Once finished, the larger box should fit easily on top of the smaller one to form your origami gift box. M&M's fit neatly inside and make a fun gift.

JOY

DECEMBER

13

Good Gifts

Every good gift and every perfect gift is from above, and cometh down from the Father of lights, with whom is no variableness, neither shadow of turning.
James 1:17 (KJV)

The closer we get to Christmas day, the more our attention turns to getting and receiving gifts. We choose to show our care and love for others by giving gifts. Maybe you make a list of things that you want because grandparents and aunts and uncles enjoy buying gifts that they know you will like. Maybe your mom keeps a list for you because your parents look for hints and listen when we share the things we want. Those who love us share our joy when we unwrap something that we love on Christmas morning. When we give gifts, we eagerly look for the reaction of joy that others will have too.

The Bible talks about giving gifts as well. We read the story of the Wise Men bringing gifts to Jesus, we read about spiritual gifts we receive to serve others, and we see in this passage from James that everything we receive—the home we live in, the car we ride in, the clothes we wear, and the sports we play—are all gifts. They are good and perfect gifts and come from our Father who loves us so much and knows just what we need. Sometimes we ask for something and don't realize that there is something better or that the thing we want might actually hurt us. We get disappointed when we don't receive what we ask for, but we can trust that our Father always gives us the very best. He knows just what we need, when we need it, and He delights to give us those things. He loves to bring us joy!

Thank you for being such a good Father to us and for showing us how much you love us!

Reflections:

Can you share a time when you asked for something but were disappointed you didn't get it?

_____

_____

_____

_____

What are some spiritual gifts you can ask God for? (Read Galatians 5:22–23)

_____

_____

_____

_____

Share a time you gave someone a gift and how it made you feel.

_____

_____

_____

_____

Let's Make A Gift! Hot Cocoa in a Jar

SUPPLIES:

- Quart mason jars with lids and bands

INGREDIENTS:

- Burlap ribbon
- Snowflake embellishments
- Colored string
- Colorful fabric
- Glue or glue dots
- Tags
- Brown craft paper
- Candy canes

Optional decorating items:
- 1 cup sugar
- 1 cup unsweetened cocoa
- 1 cup powdered milk
- ½ cup miniature marshmallows
- ½ cup chocolate chips
- ½ cup white chocolate chips
- 1-quart mason jar

DIRECTIONS:

1. Using a clean quart jar, layer the ingredients, starting with the unsweetened cocoa (it may help to use a funnel for the cocoa and sugar). Decorate the jar by tying ribbon or fabric around the lid, taping on a candy cane, or however you wish!
2. When ready to serve, pour into a bowl and stir. After using, store in an airtight container.

Tag to include with the jar:
Stir ⅓ cup of mix into one cup of hot water.
Makes 12 servings.

DECEMBER

14

Root of Jesse

⊸———⊷

And again, Esaias saith, There shall be a root of Jesse, and he that shall rise to reign over the Gentiles; in him shall the Gentiles trust. Now the God of hope fill you with all joy and peace in believing, that ye may abound in hope, through the power of the Holy Ghost. Romans 15:12–13 (KJV)

This passage reminds me of the Old Testament prophecy of the birth of Jesus. Long after Isaiah lived, the prophecy of Jesus's birth came true. The root of Jesse shows us that God continues to fulfill His promise to Abraham and David. The truth that we learn from Romans is that this same hope that the ancient Jews had that God could be trusted to keep His promises can still be trusted today. Because He is good and trustworthy, we can be filled with hope and joy and peace because of the Holy Spirit who lives in us after salvation.

Jesse was David's father, and Matthew 1 shows us how that genealogy leads to Jesus's birth. Jesus is known as the root of Jesse because he is one of his descendants. As the root of Jesse, Jesus kept the promise that one of David's relatives would always be King for the Jewish nation. When they sinned and God allowed them to be taken away to Babylon, many lost their hope and thought that maybe God had failed them after all. Instead, the prophecy came true and all those who were watching and waiting got to see God do more than they could have imagined. This baby, a direct descendent of David and heir to the throne, was the promised redemption that Isaiah knew would come.

When I am tempted to believe that God has forgotten me, or has not answered my prayers, I can trust that He is faithful. Although I might not understand His timing, He is always good and faithful to do what He has promised.

⊸———⊷

God, I thank you that you never forget me. I can rest in your promises always.

Reflections:

What promises in the Bible can I hold on to? (I John 1:9 is a good one.)

_____

_____

_____

_____

Who is it that fills me with joy according to Romans 15:12–13?

_____

_____

_____

_____

How can I be joyful with my friends and family?

_____

_____

_____

_____

Sugar Cookie Cutouts

INGREDIENTS:

- 1 cup unsalted butter
- 1 cup granulated white sugar
- 1 teaspoon vanilla extract
- ½ teaspoon almond extract
- 1 egg
- 2 teaspoons baking powder
- ½ teaspoon salt
- 3 cups all-purpose flour

DIRECTIONS:

1. Preheat oven to 350°F.
2. Cream butter and sugar until smooth.
3. Beat in extracts and egg.

4. In a separate bowl, combine baking powder and salt with flour. Add a little at a time to the wet ingredients. The dough will be very stiff. If it becomes too stiff for your mixer, turn out the dough onto a countertop surface. Wet your hands and finish off kneading the dough by hand.

5. Divide into workable batches, roll out onto a floured surface until about ¼" thick, and cut with your favorite cookie cutters.

6. Bake for 6–8 minutes. Let cool on the cookie sheet until firm enough to transfer to a cooling rack.

7. Keep in mind that the recipe yield will vary according to how thick you roll your cookies and how large or small your cutters are.

8. Frost or decorate with food-safe pens and glitters as desired.

15 *Shepherds Rejoice*

And there were in the same country shepherds abiding in the field, keeping watch over their flock by night . . . And the shepherds returned, glorifying and praising God for all the things that they had heard and seen, as it was told unto them.
Luke 2:8, 20 (KJV)

One of the key features of the Gospel is the fact that it is available to everyone. There are no restrictions on the good news message—you don't have to be very rich and you don't have to be very talented or incredibly smart. Not at all! Instead, Jesus always welcomed people who had nothing to give Him and even told the disciples to let the little children come to him! What good news this is for all of us!

Even the message of Jesus's birth was delivered to the country shepherds who were busy watching their sheep. Shepherds didn't usually get a lot of attention. They certainly weren't popular or famous. That's why it's so exciting that the birth announcement was given to them. Jesus, the Messiah, the one for whom so many were waiting, had arrived, and the responsibility for spreading the message was given to the shepherds. How exciting that the Gospel is meant for everyone, not just certain kinds of people!

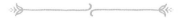

God, I praise you that the Gospel is good news for everyone who believes. Thank you for making a way for me to reach you.

Reflections:

Why is it so special that the exciting news was shared with the shepherds instead of the rulers and priests or famous people of Jesus's time?

_____

_____

_____

Are there any people that are excluded from the message of the good news?

_____

_____

_____

What does Romans 1:16 mean that "to the Jew first and also to the Greek?"

_____

_____

_____

Who should I share the good news with?

_____

_____

_____

Wood Bead Ornament

SUPPLIES:

- Wooden beads in various sizes
- Twine
- White spray paint
- Sandpaper

DIRECTIONS:

1. String the beads you plan to use for your ornaments on an extra-long piece of twine and tie it up outside somewhere you can spray paint.

2. Spray paint the beads white. After the paint is dry, sand the beads to make them look more distressed.

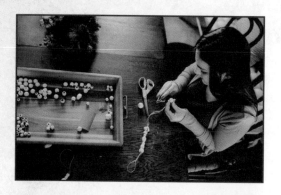

3. Cut a piece of twine about 24" long. Fold the piece of twine in half and tie a knot in the twine 3" down from where the twine is folded in half. This will be the loop that the ornament will hang from.

4. Slide both pieces of twine through your beads, creating the pattern you want with your beads. You can put the large ones in the middle and smaller ones on either side. Or large to small, small to large. Or any other combo you can think of. Tie a knot after the last bead.

5. Cut the extra twine off and hang wherever you wish.

16

Wise Men's Gifts

And when they were come into the house, they saw the young child with Mary his mother, and fell down, and worshipped him: and when they had opened their treasures, they presented unto him gifts; gold, and frankincense and myrrh. Matthew 2:11 (KJV)

Giving and receiving gifts is a big part of the Christmas season and celebrating the advent story. We all enjoy receiving a gift, especially if it's something we have really wanted for a long time. Giving gifts, though, is something that we often enjoy more and more as we get older. Listening for our friends and family to mention something they like or want and then remembering that thing and making plans to get it for a gift is so much fun! And spending time baking cookies or crafting gifts is not only fun for us but also lets others know we care.

The wise men travelled a great distance to see the king they had believed they would see, and they brought precious gifts of gold, frankincense, and myrrh. They gave from their best. They had waited and looked forward to the day they could travel to meet the king that had been promised. Today, we wait with patience and longing for the day of His return. He has promised that He will come again (John 14:1–4)!

Lord, I thank you for giving us only the very best gifts.

Reflections:

Have you listened to any of your friends and family for ideas for their gifts this year? Whose gift are you most excited to buy or make?

_____

_____

_____

What gift do you think Jesus wants from us?

_____

_____

_____

What do you think today's modern-day gold, frankincense, and myrrh gifts are?

_____

_____

_____

What does John 14:1–4 teach us about Jesus coming again?

_____

_____

_____

Button Christmas Tree

SUPPLIES:

- Buttons of various sizes and colors
- Stretchy cord string

DIRECTIONS:

1. Line up buttons by color and by size. Pick 2 or 3 brown color buttons for a trunk, and additional green buttons for the green part of the tree in order from smallest to largest.

2. Make a loop in the stretchy cord and thread the buttons through both holes to the bottom of the string. Thread the buttons through the buttonholes in order, trunk first and then the green part of the tree, largest to smallest.

3. Add a bead or star to the top if desired and tie a knot to hold it all together tightly. Then take the remainder of the cord and tie onto the real Christmas tree.

DECEMBER

17

Follow Directions

When they saw the star, they rejoiced with exceeding great joy.
Matthew 2:10 (KJV)

Do you ever look at the night sky and think, "That's awesome!" From stars to planets, and comets to meteors, the night sky is full of amazing testimony to God's creation. For centuries, men have looked to the sky for guidance. Following the movement of the stars in the sky helped people navigate across great deserts and vast plains. The location of specific stars and planets have guided those who have travelled far and long.

Long before Jesus was born, some people were watching the skies to guide them to the promised King. Old Testament prophecy had indicated that a star would appear, and wise men from the East had heard the stories passed down through generations that the Messiah would come, and a star would lead them to Him.

They had listened to the teaching, and then they acted on it, recognizing the star when it appeared and following it to find Jesus! Because they followed the star, they found the King and rejoiced that God's Word had been proven true and worthy of trust. We should all learn to not only listen but to also follow the teaching found in the Bible! Often, following directions requires listening and obeying, and sometimes it requires faith!

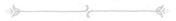

Dear Jesus, help me to always follow your directions that I can find in your Word.

Reflections:

Do you ever struggle to follow directions? If so, why?

_____

_____

_____

_____

What is your favorite star, planet, or constellation to look for in the night sky?

_____

_____

_____

_____

Read Psalm 147:4 and Genesis 15:5. What did you learn about the stars?

_____

_____

_____

_____

3D Paper Stars

SUPPLIES:

- 12 x 12 Christmas scrapbook paper or cardstock
- Paper trimmer
- Scissors
- Pencil
- Double-sided tape or paper glue

DIRECTIONS:

1. Take a square of paper and fold in half. Open out, rotate 90 degrees, and fold in half again. Open out and fold your paper in half again, this time along both diagonals.

2. Flip the paper over and mark a little less than halfway down each of the horizontal and vertical creases.

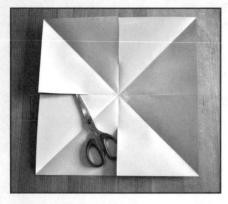

3. Cut down to the pencil marks.

4. Fold the paper in on each side of the cut to form a point. Repeat on all remaining sides.

5. Apply glue or double-sided tape to one side of each of the points. Fold one side of the point over the other and stick down. Do the same on the remaining points to make half a star. Repeat the steps above to make the second half. Apply some more glue to the center corners of each point.

6. Stick both halves together, making sure the points are at 45 degrees from each other.

7. Leave to dry, then hang.

DECEMBER

18   *Joy and Suffering*

Looking unto Jesus the author and finisher of our faith; who for the joy that was set before him endured the cross, despising the shame, and is set down at the right hand of the throne of God. Hebrews 12:2 (KJV)

One of the mysteries of understanding the coming of Jesus, the promised Messiah, and His death and resurrection is trying to reconcile the joy of the Christmas season with the suffering and pain that comes later in Jesus's story. Without the suffering of Jesus, the payment for our sins could not be made. It can be difficult to understand how looking forward to the cross brought Jesus joy. It brings joy to us in knowing that this great gift was given, but I often struggle with the description that I read here of the joy set before Him. Jesus knew His purpose was death on the cross and chose to come to us anyway.

To me this means that the joy was understanding how great this gift really was—this gift of reconciling or repairing the way of man to reach God. He is holy and we are not. He is perfect and we are not. Jesus was the only One who could make that way for us. But it cost Him a very high price.

The gifts we give each other pale in comparison, but every time I give a gift that requires a small sacrifice, it's quite meaningful to me. I find so much joy in the giving that I can barely hold it in. Keeping the secret of a really fun gift can be so hard!

It gave Jesus joy to give His life, because He knew it was the only way to restore our relationship with God. What an incredible gift!

Dear Lord, I thank you for the joy that we share because Jesus came to earth.

Reflections:

Have you ever had to make a sacrifice to be able to give someone a gift?

_____

_____

_____

_____

How could you sacrifice your time this week to make someone feel special?

_____

_____

_____

_____

What does Isaiah 43:2 promise me about suffering?

_____

_____

_____

_____

Peppermint Candy Ornaments

SUPPLIES:

- Peppermint candies
- Metal cookie cutters
- Nonstick cooking spray
- Parchment paper

DIRECTIONS:

1. Preheat the oven to 350°F.
2. Line a baking sheet with parchment paper. Spray the insides of metal cookie cutters with cooking spray.
3. Arrange peppermint candies inside the cookie cutters, leaving a little space between the candies.
4. Bake for 5–6 minutes. Watch closely and remove from the oven once the candies are melted. Cool for one minute and make a small hole in the top of the candy with a greased skewer.
5. Cool completely and gently pop the candies out of the cookie cutters. Be gentle! It's best to gently pull the metal cookie cutter away from the peppermint ornament before popping out.

JOY 77

PEACE

DECEMBER

19

Gospel of Peace

And your feet shod with the preparation of the gospel of peace. Ephesians 6:15 (KJV)

We prepare our hearts and our homes for Christmas each year. The preparation might mean cleaning some areas for company to come and stay. It might mean extra work to get the garage or attic cleaned up before we bring down (or up) the decorations that we use for Christmas each year. Preparing our home for guests to arrive requires extra time, extra work, and extra attention to detail.

Preparing our hearts for this season is important as well. We need to get rid of the junk in our hearts, too! We should prepare our hearts with good attitudes for celebrating the real reason for our celebration this season. Removing our selfishness and seeking to put others and their needs first is an important part of preparing for Christmas. Putting others first, we will see more easily the needs that others have and choose to work to meet those needs.

This passage reminds me that we must prepare in advance to spread the gospel, the good news that the Prince of Peace came into the world to rescue us. We should prepare ourselves by reading the Bible and praying so we will have the right words to say when we have opportunities to tell others about Jesus and the good news!

Thank you, God, for being our peace. Help me share that same peace with others.

Reflections:

What does peace mean to you?

_____

_____

_____

_____

What does peace look like to you?

_____

_____

_____

_____

What does Psalm 34:14 tell us to do?

_____

_____

_____

_____

Mason Jar Luminaries

SUPPLIES:

- Mason jar (or any glass jar)
- 1 cup of Epsom salt
- 1 tablespoon glitter (preferably white or translucent)
- Mod Podge (or tacky glue)

- Sponge brush for applying the glue
- Clear adhesive spray
- Twine or ribbon
- Hot glue gun
- Flameless tea lights or fairy string lights

DIRECTIONS:

1. Mix Epsom salt and glitter together in a bowl.
2. With a sponge brush, apply a thin, even layer of Mod Podge onto the outside of the jar. Be careful not to use too much or it will drip.
3. Cover your working area with newspaper and immediately pour or spoon over the Epsom salt mixture until all of the glue has been fully covered; set aside to dry for about an hour. Spray with clear adhesive to protect the surface.

4. Wrap and tie twine or ribbon around until you have your desired look.
5. Add tea lights or even small fairy string lights to the inside and watch them glow.

DECEMBER

20 *Good Tidings of Great Joy*

And the angel said unto them, Fear not: for, behold, I bring you good tidings of great joy, which shall be to all people. For unto you is born this day in the city of David a Saviour, which is Christ the Lord. Luke 2:10–11 (KJV)

One of the problems with being fearful is the fact that fear steals our peace. Peace and calm can be so hard to find, but the promise of Christ's birth and ultimately His presence with us brings an instant sense of peace. Going to school, practicing an instrument or sport, and doing homework can be hard, especially when something is difficult to understand. But I know that no matter what, I can still have peace. Jesus lived life just as we do today. He was a toddler and a teenager. He was a student and a teacher. He had to study and learn, and yet He did it all without sinning.

When I am struggling, He is present.

When I am hurt, He is my comfort.

When I am sad, He is my joy.

When I am overwhelmed, He is my calm.

There is nothing that I face today that I need to fear. The message of Jesus's birth is still good and it fills us with great joy, even today.

Thank you, God, that I do not need to fear. You have everything and everyone under your control for my good and your glory.

Reflections:

Tell about a time when you were afraid.

_____

_____

_____

_____

What can you do today to bring more peace to your home?

_____

_____

_____

_____

What does Proverbs 12:20 say about peace? What do you think it means?

_____

_____

_____

_____

Simple DIY Nativity Story Stones

SUPPLIES:

- Smooth surface stones
- Black craft pens (choose water resistant pens that write on a variety of surfaces)
- Chalk pens
- Mod Podge glue (optional)

DIRECTIONS:

1. Draw the outlines of the characters in black pen. You can do as many characters from the Nativity story as you like, but at least have Mary, Joseph, and baby Jesus.

2. Use the chalk pens to fill in the black outlines.

3. For extra staying power, cover with Mod Podge and allow to fully dry. Use the stones to tell the story of Jesus's birth over and over again.

DECEMBER

21

Fear Not

And the angel said unto her, Fear not, Mary: for thou hast found favour with God. Luke 1:30 (KJV)

$\mathcal{M}$ary had so much to be scared about. She was going to be a first-time mom, she was betrothed or engaged to marry Joseph in a short time, and her life was being completely turned upside down. She must have been so fearful of this news that the angel brought her. So the angel made sure to reassure her and tell her not to fear! He knew that she must be so frightened with the news that he had shared, so he told her that this was actually good news. She had been specially chosen by God to be Jesus's mom.

It doesn't matter if you have fears about a test in school or moving to a new house in a new town, we all have fears that we must face. We can be afraid of the dark, of having an accident, and of so many other things. But there are many times in the Bible that we are assured that we don't have to fear, because God is with us. My favorite verse in the Bible is, "What time I am afraid I will trust in thee" (Psalm 56:3). This is a short verse that you can memorize and recite anytime you are worried or afraid. Trusting the truth of God's Word helps us in those times when we are filled with fear. In these times we learn to trust instead.

Thank you, Lord, that when I am afraid, I can pray and trust you with every fear. I thank you for hearing me when I call.

Reflections:

What do you imagine Mary thought when the angel told her the news? How did she feel?

_____

_____

_____

_____

Read Psalm 4:8. Share what this verse teaches you. Memorize it and Psalm 56:3 so that you can remind yourself of these truths when you are afraid.

_____

_____

_____

_____

Read Psalm 118:6 and Hebrews 13:6. What should we not fear?

_____

_____

_____

_____

Let's Make a Gift! Peppermint Sugar Scrub

SUPPLIES:

- 2 cups sugar
- ⅔ cup coconut oil
- 15 drops of peppermint essential oil
- 16 oz. wide mouth mason jar
- Printable gift tag

DIRECTIONS:

1. Melt coconut oil in the microwave. Test after 30 seconds and continue for 15 seconds at a time until melted.
2. Mix sugar and coconut oil together.
3. Add 15 drops of peppermint essential oil and mix with spatula.
4. Fill the mason jar with the peppermint sugar scrub.
5. This recipe will fill one 16-ounce mason jar.
6. After the jar is filled, attach the label to the jar along with any decoration you would like.

DECEMBER

22

Peace on Earth

Glory to God in the highest, and on earth peace, good will toward men.
Luke 2:14 (KJV)

The world can be a noisy place. Sometimes there are lots of voices that seem angry, or people who are unhappy and complaining. During the Christmas season, sometimes the feelings that people have year-round can overflow because of the stress of trying to do all the activities and make everything just right. We all long for peace—calm, quiet, and the sense that everything will be all right.

One night long ago, the world stopped for a little while and pondered with wonder what the angels were saying. They proclaimed that peace had come to earth. Peace in the gift of a baby. Peace in the form of God who became man and came to dwell with us. And this wonderful, glorious, good news is that we can still know that same peace today. Both in the knowledge of our salvation, but also in the way we live our lives day to day. Instead of being driven along with the hurry and fury of the day, we can choose to cling to Jesus and rest in the peace that He brings when we trust Him to handle every need.

I thank you Lord once again for sending peace to us as a little baby. Thank you that we can celebrate peace this Christmas because of Jesus.

Reflections:

How can you help bring peace into your home this Christmas?

_____

_____

_____

_____

Do you think that patience and peace work together?

_____

_____

_____

_____

Read Colossians 3:14–16. What can we learn from these verses about peace?

_____

_____

_____

_____

Homemade Marshmallows

INGREDIENTS:

- 3 packages unflavored gelatin
- 1 cup ice cold water (divided)
- 12 ounces granulated sugar
- 1 cup light corn syrup
- ¼ teaspoon kosher salt

- 1 teaspoon vanilla extract
- ¼ cup confectioners' sugar
- ¼ cup cornstarch
- Nonstick spray

DIRECTIONS:

1. In the bowl of a stand mixer, combine the gelatin with ½ cup of the cold water. Have the whisk attachment standing by.
2. Combine the remaining ½ cup water, granulated sugar, corn syrup, and salt in a 2-quart saucepan. Place over medium high heat, cover, and allow to cook for 3–4 minutes. Uncover, clip a candy thermometer onto the side of the pan, and continue to cook until the mixture reaches 240°F, approximately 7–8 minutes. When the mixture reaches this temperature, immediately remove from the heat.

3. Turn the mixer fitted with the whisk attachment to low speed and, while running, slowly pour the sugar syrup down the side of the bowl into the gelatin mixture. Once you have added all of the syrup, increase the speed to high. Continue to whip until the mixture becomes very thick and is lukewarm, approximately 12–15 minutes. Add the vanilla during the last minute of whipping.

4. While the mixture is whipping, prepare the pans as follows: Combine the confectioners' sugar and cornstarch in a small bowl. Lightly spray a 13x9-inch metal baking pan with nonstick cooking spray. Add the sugar and cornstarch mixture and move around to completely coat the bottom and sides of the pan. Return the remaining mixture to the bowl for later use.

5. When ready, pour the mixture into the prepared pan, using a lightly oiled spatula for spreading evenly into the pan. Dust the top with enough of the remaining sugar and cornstarch mixture to lightly cover. Reserve the rest for later. Allow the marshmallows to sit uncovered for at least 4 hours and up to overnight.

6. Turn the marshmallows out onto a cutting board and cut into 1-inch squares using a pizza wheel or knife dusted with the confectioners' sugar mixture.

7. Once cut, lightly dust all sides of each marshmallow with the remaining mixture, using additional if necessary. Store in an airtight container for up to 3 weeks. For a delightful serving variation, melt chocolate and dip the marshmallows in the chocolate. You can top with crushed nuts, crushed peppermint candies, or cover in sprinkles. Yum!

DECEMBER

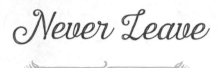

23

Never Leave

Let your conversation be without covetousness; and be content with such things as ye have: for he hath said, I will never leave thee, nor forsake thee. Hebrews 13:5 (KJV)

The verse above is one of my favorites. It fills me with peace! There are many verses throughout the Bible that assure us that God will never leave us. The reminder in this verse comes with an additional warning. The verse warns us to not be covetous, or to want what other people have.

What a good reminder during this Christmas season to be content with the gifts He has already given us and to be grateful for all the things we do have *because He has provided them.* With contentment we can have peace. Being grateful for all the blessings helps us to live our lives with compassion for others and with the proper view of gifts and gift giving, especially during this season.

In the Bible we see that Jesus is the peace in the midst of the storms with the disciples, the faithful healer of the sick and hurting, and the truth teacher in the temple. In the good and the bad, we can have peace. In the rain and the sunshine we can have rest. In all of the seasons we are blessed.

Thank you, Lord, for the promise that you never ever leave us alone. I can be at rest and peaceful because you are faithful to keep your promises.

Reflections:

What is your favorite season?

_____

_____

_____

How do you feel when you read that God will never leave you?

_____

_____

_____

II Corinthians 4:8–10 talks about not being forsaken even though we do go through trials and troubles. How can you encourage someone with these verses who might be going through a hard time?

_____

_____

_____

Read Judges 6:23–24. What does "Jehovah shalom" mean?

_____

_____

_____

Lighted Burlap Garland

SUPPLIES:

- Clear 100 white mini lights
- Burlap ribbon (90 feet)
- Scissors

DIRECTIONS:

1. Cut the burlap into 8–10-inch pieces. Then cut those pieces down the middle so that the ribbon is half as wide.
2. Tie burlap strips once around the wire.
3. Repeat until complete.

24

Listen Up!

And in the sixth month the angel Gabriel was sent from God unto a city of Galilee, named Nazareth, to a virgin espoused to a man whose name was Joseph, of the house of David; and the virgin's name was Mary. Luke 1:26–27 (KJV)

Parents and children often have difficulty talking to each other. Many times we each speak to each other without really listening; it can be hard to really stop and pay attention. Sometimes we don't listen because we are thinking of what we want to say instead. Learning to listen requires us to be quiet, to give others the opportunity to say what they need to say, and to try to see their point of view even if we disagree or dislike what we hear.

Can you imagine what young Mary must have thought when the angel came to tell her that she would be carrying a baby and that He would be the promised child? She may have had her own hopes and dreams, she may have even had her own life planned out, and this surely wasn't part of her plan. But instead of arguing, or talking over the angel, she listened and heard the promise given to her. Because she listened, she was at peace with the news the angel brought her.

If she hadn't been prepared to listen and receive the message, she might have missed out on the amazing blessing and honor that she received by being the mother of our savior.

Thank you, Jesus, for all the people involved in the Nativity story. Most of all we thank you for being our savior and rescuing us from our sins.

Reflections:

Which is harder, listening or communicating your ideas/frustrations to someone else?

_____

_____

_____

_____

How do we learn to listen better?

_____

_____

_____

_____

What does James 1:19–23 teach us about listening/hearing?

_____

_____

_____

_____

Popsicle Stick Snowflake Ornaments

SUPPLIES:

- 6–8 popsicle sticks
- 4–6-inch piece of twine or string
- Hot glue gun and glue
- Optional: acrylic paint, puffy paint, stickers, pom poms, or other small decorations

DIRECTIONS:

1. If desired, paint popsicle sticks whatever color(s) you choose. Allow to dry fully.
2. Tie a knot in the base of the twine or string. At the top and back of your bottom popsicle stick, put a little hot glue and attach the knotted end of the string very carefully.
3. After it has dried, turn the popsicle stick over and put a dot of hot glue in the center. Attach the next popsicle stick going across horizontally.
4. Repeat with the remaining popsicle sticks, staggering the angles as you add more sticks.
5. Decorate as desired with stickers, pom poms, puffy paint, etc.!

Craft Supply List by Week

WEEK ONE
GROCERY STORE LIST:

- 1 cup flour
- 1 teaspoon baking powder
- ⅓ cup light brown sugar, packed
- ½ cup granulated sugar
- ½ cup + ¼ teaspoon salt
- ½ teaspoon baking soda
- 1½ cups all-purpose flour
- 1¼ cups holiday M&Ms
- Cooking spray
- Food coloring
- Plastic straw
- Recipe card
- Recycled plastic (any clear plastic—fruit containers are great!)
- 1-quart Mason jar

CRAFT STORE LIST:

- Glue
- Green yarn
- Curling ribbon
- Jute (optional)
- Mini pom poms or buttons
- Paint brush
- Puffy paint
- Sharpies
- Yellow card scraps
- Acrylic paint
- Baker's twine (optional)
- Black construction paper
- Cinnamon sticks (optional)
- Clear spray paint to seal ornaments
- Colorful tissue paper
- Contact paper
- 2 pounds oatmeal soap base

TOOLS:

- Glue gun and glue
- Scissors
- Soap molds

OTHER:

- 2 teaspoons cinnamon bark essential oil
- Nativity silhouette (hand drawn or printed from computer)
- Varying sizes of sticks/twigs

WEEK TWO
GROCERY STORE LIST:

- 1 cup chocolate chips
- 1 teaspoon vanilla extract
- ½ cup peanut butter
- ¼ cup butter
- 2 cups powdered sugar
- 2 cups red and green M&Ms
- 7 cups Chex cereal
- Cotton balls

CRAFT STORE LIST:

- 2 pieces of square paper (recycled Christmas cards are perfect!)
- 1 green or brown popsicle stick
- 3 green popsicle sticks
- Craft glue
- Construction paper (Christmas colors, and black)
- Googly eyes
- Foam star stickers
- Ribbons
- Sparkly stickers for ornaments
- 2 mini clothespins
- Twine, string or cord

TOOLS:

- Hot glue gun & glue
- Pen, pencil, marker, or crayon
- Scissors
- String and needle
- Tape or stapler and staples
- Sharpie marker

OTHER:

- Straight sticks or cinnamon sticks

WEEK THREE
GROCERY STORE LIST:
- 2 cup granulated white sugar
- 1 cup powdered milk
- 1 cup unsalted butter
- 1 cup unsweetened cocoa
- 1 egg
- 1 teaspoon vanilla extract
- ½ teaspoon almond extract
- ½ teaspoon salt
- ½ cup chocolate chips
- ½ cup miniature marshmallows
- ½ cup white chocolate chips
- 2 teaspoons baking powder
- 3 cups all-purpose flour
- Candy canes
- Nonstick cooking spray
- Parchment Paper
- Peppermint candies
- 1-quart mason jars w/lids and bands

CRAFT STORE LIST:
- Brown craft paper
- Burlap ribbon
- Buttons of various sizes and colors
- 12 x 12 Christmas scrapbook paper or cardstock
- Snowflakes embellishments
- Stretchy cord string
- Gift tags
- Twine
- White spray paint
- Wooden beads in various sizes
- Colored string
- Colorful fabric
- Double-sided tape or paper glue
- Glue or glue dots

TOOLS:
- Scissors
- Paper trimmer
- Pencil

OTHER:
- Metal cookie cutters
- Sandpaper

WEEK FOUR
GROCERY STORE LIST:
- 1 cup light corn syrup
- 1 cup Epsom salt
- 1 teaspoon vanilla extract
- ¼ cup confectioners' sugar
- ¼ cup cornstarch
- ¼ teaspoon kosher salt
- 12 ounces granulated sugar
- 2 cups sugar
- ⅔ cup coconut oil
- 3 packages unflavored gelatin
- 16 oz. wide mouth mason jar
- Additional Mason jar (or any glass jar)
- Nonstick spray

CRAFT STORE LIST:
- 1 tablespoon glitter (preferably white or translucent)
- Black craft pens (choose water resistant pens that write on a variety of surfaces)
- Burlap ribbon in natural, red, and green (30 feet of each ribbon)
- Chalk pens
- Clear 100 white mini lights
- Clear adhesive spray
- Mod podge (or tacky glue)
- Printable gift tag
- Small piece of greenery
- Sponge brush for applying the glue
- Tea lights or fairy string lights
- Various sizes & colors popsicle sticks
- Twine
- Puffy & acrylic paint
- Stickers
- Pom poms

TOOLS:
- Hot glue gun
- Scissors

OTHER:
- Smooth surface stones
- 15 drops peppermint essential oil

Acknowledgments

Special thanks to:

Josie Siler and family, photographer, @JosieSiler on Facebook

Casey Bender Butler and family, photographer, @caseybphotography79 on Facebook

Linde Lightkep and family, photographer, @LindeLouPhotography on Facebook

Naomi McIntosh and family, photographer, @naomimcintoshphotography on Facebook

Mary Beth Barrows, @smallcakespensacola on Facebook

Stephanie Gilbert, @msstephaniegilbert on Instagram

Jessica, @reefrainaria on Instagram

Kelly Radcliff, @thetatteredpew on Instagram

And a big thank you to the families who helped with craft projects!

Doug & Christy Douglas and family

Cyle & Patty Young and family

Jonathan & Kim Wood and family

Joe & Bridget McClellan and family